A Mother's Bouquet

Fragrant Reminiscences
of Mom with Four Scents

**Andrews McMeel
Publishing**

Kansas City

by Julie Merberg   Illustrations by Sandy Haight

For my mom—JM

ISBN: 0-7407-4218-3

02 03 04 05 06 LF 10 9 8 7 6 5 4 3 2 1

Printed in China

A Roundtable Press Book

Directors: Julie Merberg and Marsha Melnick

Design by pink design, inc. (www.pinkdesigninc.com)

Illustrations by Sandy Haight (www.sandyhaight.com)

Research by Sara Newberry and Marian Makins

Whether your mother's personal bouquet exudes **home-cooked meals** or leather attachés; whether she was **spick-and-span** or splattered with marinara sauce; whether she **smoked** or chewed peppermints; whether she favored **unscented soap** or left a cloud of perfume in her wake . . . the scent of certain things your mom wore, cooked, created, or simply surrounded herself with, is indelibly marked in your olfactory cells.

3

The scents of our mothers—from her face cream to her favorite flower—envelop us from the moment we leave the womb; reassure us as children; and bring us back to a safe, warm place whenever we catch a whiff of perfume, chocolate chip cookies, cheap white wine, lavender, expensive wool . . . or whatever other scents evoke our own moms.

The sense of smell is our keenest sense, the one that brings memories into sharp focus;  makes food appealing, irresistible, or repugnant; and even drives our attraction to other people. We are born with a highly developed sense of smell. Seconds after birth, a baby placed on his mother's chest will move to the breast and begin to suckle. The baby is responding to the smell emanating from his mother's breast, which is reminiscent of the taste of amniotic fluid consumed in utero.

From the very beginning, a mother's unique scent holds the power to make us feel secure and loved.

Within a few days of birth, a newborn baby can select her own mother's scent over that of other mothers. A baby might even refuse to nurse if her mother smells different—if she uses a new soap or perfume. Breast-feeding mothers will leave an infant with a well-worn shirt to comfort the baby and coax him into taking a bottle from another caregiver. From the very beginning, a mother's unique scent holds the power to make us feel secure and loved.

Interestingly enough, the scent-bond runs both ways. Mothers find the smell of their own kids' diapers oddly pleasant (or at least not offensive). But changing another child's diaper is extremely unappealing!

Newborns instinctively like sweet tastes and smells. They can distinguish breast milk (which is naturally high in sugar) from any other liquid, and will take sugar water over plain water. Babies will breathe deeply if they catch a whiff of milk, banana, vanilla, or sugar—but sour or bitter scents like vinegar or alcohol will make them wrinkle their little noses.

Smell was the first of our senses, and it was so successful that in time the small bump of olfactory tissue atop the nerve cord grew into a brain. Our cerebral hemispheres were originally buds from the olfactory stalks. We think because we smelled.

Diane Ackerman,
A Natural History of the Senses

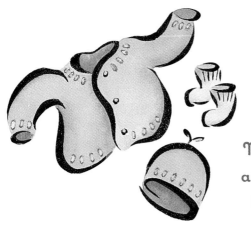

A young child knows
Mother as a smelled skin,
a halo of light, a strength
in the arms, a voice that
trembles with feeling,

Annie Dillard,
An American Childhood

Research has shown that our first exposure to an
odor determines our feelings about that particular smell—
which will always evoke the happiness, melancholy,
arousal, anger, or whatever other emotions are entwined
with that experience.

The nursery is a quiet,
cozy, pastel, padded haven
where a new mom goes
to drink in her baby and the
new, yet familiar odors:
diaper ointment,
golden baby wash,
mild, pink lotion,
and a sprinkling of powder...

smell the baby powder!

From the nursery to the office or studio, the garden to the kitchen, mothers are, above all else, creators and nurturers. For this reason, even if she didn't have a green thumb, raise her own herbs in a window box, or plant seeds after the last frost, Mom is still celebrated with flowers.

The carnation is the traditional Mother's Day flower, with colored carnations indicating that a mother is living, and white carnations that she is deceased. But anything goes—gardenias, roses, tulips, or a bouquet of fresh spring blossoms. Whatever makes her smile.

12

I could not figure out why my mother made such a fuss about a handful of pots that sat for months doing nothing . . . The first flower was a big moment. At dinner, it was the centerpiece. When relatives came, it was trundled into some highly visible position. But pretty soon, daffodils, muscari, and hyacinths were so plentiful they were relegated to the kitchen table where they overlooked the preparation of apple pies and witnessed after-school milk being spilled all over the cookies . . . By the time they were in bloom—and the tulips always lagged behind everything else—they were no longer the great sensation . . . There was something wonderful about that, about walking by the daffodils and being so familiar with their company, you forgot to bury your nose in them.

Tovah Martin,
A Time to Blossom

My mother smelled of
laundered cretonne,
of irons heated on
the poplar-wood fire,
of lemon-verbena
leaves which she rolled
between her palms or thrust into her pocket.
At nightfall I used to imagine that she smelled
of newly-watered lettuces, for the refreshing scent
of them would follow her footsteps to the rippling
sound of the rain from the watering-can, in a
glory of spray and tillable dust.

Colette,
My Mother's House

14

[My mother] had a fine sense of color, and a passion for scented flowers. Soon I would drift off to sleep in the evening bathed in the perfume of stocks, wallflowers, and heliotrope in summer, the crisp aroma of chrysanthemums in autumn. A whole bed was given over to Parma violets, and great fistfuls of them would sit in the middle of the round table on which we dined in summer on the southern screened veranda.

Jill Ker Conway,
The Road from Coorain

A great lawn sloped north from the building down to a seawall and a narrow beach . . . Flower beds had been planted along the building's east side, and I remember walking in them with my mother to pick flowers as tall as I was. I remember the aroma of the soil in summer and the way the bare earth puckered to a dry crust after an early morning watering.

The odor and the flowers' colors in the garden attracted me. To ensure visits there with Mother, I'd sometimes line my alphabet blocks up on a windowsill—our windows were right above the gardens—and push them out. She'd take me along to retrieve them while she gathered bouquets.

Barry Lopez,
About This Life

Blessed is the memory of an old-fashioned mother. It floats to us now like the beautiful perfume from some wooded blossoms.

Rosella A. Thorne,
Treasury of Thought:
Mother, Home, and Heaven

17

Let us be grateful
to people who
make us happy:
They are the charming
gardeners who
make our souls
bloom.

Marcel Proust

smell the gardenias!

I remember good days for the shared pleasure we took in them—family expeditions to pick berries in the Cypress Hills, when we picnicked on the edge of Chimney Coulee and watched great fleets of clouds sail eastward over the prairie.

Raising a sandwich to your mouth, you exclaimed, "Oh! Smell your hands!" and we did, inhaling the fragrance of the saskatoons, gooseberries, chokecherries, pin cherries, and highbush cranberries we had been working on . . . You never lost an opportunity to sing. You sang, too, among the rich smells in the kitchen as you made those wild berries into pies and jams and sauces and jellies and put a lot of them up in jars and glasses to be stored on the cellar shelves.

Wallace Stegner,
Where the Bluebird Sings to the Lemonade Springs: Living and Writing in the West

Old enough to stand on two feet, we left our mothers' arms and our noses were no longer pressed up against her neck or buried in her hair. Instead, we could take in her whole environment— the lingering scent of shampoo when she brushed her hair, the perfume she spritzed or dabbed, the lavender sachets that kept her clothes smelling like a garden.

Mama's perfume is a scent that was created for her by Claude Hovet, the *parfumier* in the French Quarter, when she was sixteen. A gift from Genevieve Whitman, it is a scent that is softly shocking and deeply moving. A scent that disturbs me and delights me. It smells like ripe pears, vetiver, a bit of violet, and something else—something spicy, almost biting and exotic . . . I live in an ocean of smell, and the ocean is my mother.

Rebecca Wells,
Divine Secrets of the Ya-Ya Sisterhood

And who does not remember the pretty things that mother wore! Her dainty laces, the pale lilac dresses, the scent of violets, the rose tucked under the lace on her breast, seem half divine when they become but memories to us.

Rosella A. Thorne,
*Treasury of Thought:
Mother, Home, and Heaven*

Chanel № 5. When I was growing up, my mother always wore Chanel № 5. Everything about it reminds me of her: its light floral sting, the cold, smooth weight of the rectangular bottle, the crystal stopper that she used to dab the perfume, first on her neck, then mine, thus anointing me. When I detect the scent on someone else, I can't help but think "pretender!" before reason wrestles childhood id to the ground. And although I don't wear it myself, I keep a bottle on my dresser (after all, how often does one get the chance to express daughterly fealty via beauty product?).

To this day, even when I'm walking through the sickly atmospheric vapor of department store spritzers, I can almost always find the fragrant, soothing curl of Chanel № 5 in the ether—turning, stretching, pointing the way home so I won't be late for dinner.

Ellen Tien

24

My own mother, moving gracefully through the house and garden, arranging flowers, breakfasting on a white wicker tray in her bedroom, was easily the most beautiful creature imaginable. She was Maureen O'Sullivan, a famous movie star, and her voice was soft with a light Irish accent. She seemed possessed of magical qualities, an unending supply of stories, and the ability to make me feel safe and happy. She was, of course, unaware of her own perfection or the unsettling, elusive quality that could flood me with yearning and loneliness. At night I lay in bed listening for the rustle of silk or taffeta, waiting for her perfume to overpower the scent of jasmine.

Mia Farrow,
What Falls Away

I turned . . . and entered the invisible cloud of odors that floated around Mother at that time: Shalimar and tobacco and peppermint Life Savers. For some reason, I recall it drifting just above my head, which moved at the level of her hipbone, so I could crane my head up and breath deeply and draw some of her down into my lungs.

Mary Karr,
The Liars' Club

The woman of that time cut a handsome figure, with a fine head of hair, which she dyed red . . . She wore turbans and had two favorite dresses, a summer one with big, blue stripes and a soft, beige one made of seersucker. She powdered her face with a puff in a mirror above the sink and dabbed perfume behind her ear. When she put on lipstick, she always started with the heart-shaped bit in the middle. She turned to face the wall when she fastened her corset. Her flesh bulged through the crisscross of laces, joined together at her waist by a knot and a small rosette. I knew every detail of her body. I thought that I would grow up to become her.

Annie Ernaux,
A Woman's Story

Mom's perfume enters a room before she does, and lingers long after she leaves it.

smell the perfume!

I adored an old lady who smelled always of lemon verbena sachet. I slept with her and cozied in the dark. Often she would say, "Bring up the chair, darling, and climb to the top drawer of the bureau," and there I would find some goody. A little cupcake, or once, to my delight, some kumquats. This first love was my grandmother, whom I called Mommy.

Carson McCullers,
*Illumination and Night Glare:
The Unfinished Autobiography of
Carson McCullers*

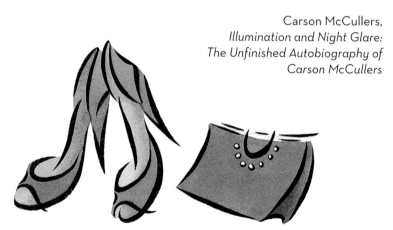

Every night,
I go into the
living room to say my prayers out loud
for Momma . . . After prayers, she kisses
me good night and gives me a hug.
It's the best kind of hug with our faces
cheek to cheek and the smell of her
almond lotion.

Jennifer Lauck,
Blackbird: A Childhood Lost and Found

Some mothers cook. Some mothers buy.
All mothers feed their children.
Comfort foods—the soul-warming,
satisfying fare that makes the world's
worries float away like steam
off a pot of chicken soup—
mean different things to
different people.

Like mom used to make . . .

LATINO	beans and rice, fried plantains
GREEK	moussaka, avgolemeno (chicken, egg & lemon soup), spanakopita
ITALIAN	meatballs with gravy, pasta
AFRICAN-AMERICAN	soul food: fried chicken, mashed potatoes, barbecue, collard greens
SOUTHERN	pecan pie, cornbread, biscuits and gravy, grits
CHINESE	steamed pork dumplings
KOREAN	rice cakes, ramen, noodles with black bean sauce
INDIAN	*chai* (tea with spices and milk), rice and dal, vegetable curry
MEXICAN	*pan dulce* with hot chocolate
MALAYSIAN	Hainese chicken rice
CAJUN	gumbo (seafood or chicken and andouille), jambalaya, cracklins

Nearly every day an echo of my mother's mothering wafts by me, like the aroma of soup simmering on a stove down the street.

Anna Quindlen,
Living Out Loud

[My mother] was taste-blind and unafraid of rot.
"Oh, it's just a little mold," I can remember her saying
on the many occasions she scraped the fuzzy blue stuff
off some concoction before serving what was left for
dinner. She had an iron stomach and was incapable of
understanding that other people did not.

This taught me many things. The first was that food
could be dangerous, especially to those who loved it.
I took this very seriously. My parents entertained a great
deal, and before I was ten I had appointed myself
guardian of the guests. My mission was to keep Mom from
killing anybody who came for dinner.

Ruth Reichl,
Tender at the Bone

Nothing cures
a cold or warms
the soul
like Mom's
chicken soup.

Chicken Noodle Soup

16 cups canned reduced-sodium chicken broth
1   whole chicken (3½ pounds), cut into 8 pieces
½   cup chopped onion
2   carrots, peeled and thinly sliced
2   ribs celery, sliced
2   tablespoons (¼ stick) butter
1   cup sliced mushrooms
1   tablespoon fresh lemon juice
½   pound dry wide egg noodles
½   cup finely chopped fresh parsley
    Salt and black pepper

36

1. Combine broth and chicken in large heavy pot. Bring just to boiling. Reduce heat; cover partially and simmer until chicken is cooked through, about 20 minutes.

2. Using tongs, transfer chicken to large bowl. Cool chicken and broth slightly. Discard skin and bones from chicken. Cut chicken meat into bite-size pieces and reserve. Spoon fat off top of broth. (Can be prepared 1 day ahead. Cover chicken meat and broth separately and refrigerate. Bring broth to boiling before continuing.)

3. Return broth to simmer. Add onion, carrots, and celery. Simmer until vegetables soften, about 8 minutes.

4. Melt butter in heavy large skillet over medium-high heat. Add mushrooms and sauté until beginning to brown, about 5 minutes. Stir in lemon juice. Add mushrooms to broth; stir in noodles, parsley, and reserved chicken. Simmer until noodles are tender, about 5 minutes. Season soup to taste with salt and pepper.

Makes 12 servings.

Mom's apple pie,
cinnamon-kissed,
with flaky crust
makes all the worries
in the world melt away...
like a scoop of vanilla
ice cream on a hot slice.

scratch and sniff the pie!

Apple Pie

1 package (15-ounces) prepared piecrusts

2¼ pounds tart green apples (such as Granny Smith), peeled, cored, and sliced

½ cup granulated sugar

¼ cup light-brown sugar

2 tablespoons plus 1 teaspoon all-purpose flour

¾ teaspoon ground cinnamon

¼ cup (½ stick) unsalted butter, cut into small pieces

1. Position rack in center of oven and heat to 400°. Place baking sheet on rack.

2. Combine apples, sugars, 2 tablespoons flour, and cinnamon in large bowl; mix to blend well.

3. Meanwhile, let piecrusts stand at room temperature 15 minutes. Unfold piecrusts and press out fold lines. Sprinkle 1 crust with remaining teaspoon flour. Place crust floured side down in 9-inch deep-dish glass pie plate.

4. Spoon apple filling into crust-lined dish. Dot filling with butter. Arrange second crust over filling. Seal and crimp edges. Cut 5 slits in top crust for steam vents.

5. Place pie on baking sheet in oven. Bake until crust is golden brown and apples are tender, about 50 minutes. If edges begin to brown too quickly, cover with aluminum foil for the remainder of baking time. Cool pie on wire rack at least 15 minutes before serving. Serve warm or at room temperature.

Makes 8 servings.

Chocolate Chip Cookies

1   cup packed golden-brown sugar
½   cup granulated sugar
1   cup (2 sticks) unsalted butter, at room temperature
2   eggs
1   teaspoon vanilla
3   cups all-purpose flour
1   teaspoon baking soda
1   teaspoon salt
1   package (12-ounce) semisweet chocolate chips
1   package (6-ounce) walnuts or pecans (optional)

1. Heat oven to 350°. Using electric mixer, beat sugars and butter in large bowl until light and fluffy. Beat in eggs, one at a time, and vanilla.

2. Mix flour, baking soda, and salt in large bowl. Add dry ingredients to butter mixture and mix until blended. Stir in chocolate chips (and nuts, if desired).

3. Drop dough by heaping tablespoonfuls onto heavy large baking sheets, spacing 2 inches apart.

4. Bake until golden brown, about 12 minutes, turning baking sheets halfway through baking. Transfer baking sheets to wire racks; cool 5 minutes. Transfer cookies to wire racks; cool completely.

Makes about 3 dozen cookies.

Macaroni and Cheese

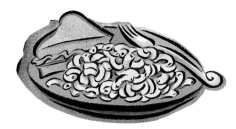

³/₄   pound dry elbow macaroni

For topping:

2   tablespoons unsalted butter

1   cup (about 4 ounces) coarsely grated extra-sharp cheddar cheese

For cheese sauce:

3   tablespoons unsalted butter

3   tablespoons all-purpose flour

3½ cups whole milk

4   cups (about 1 pound) coarsely grated extra sharp cheddar cheese

3   teaspoons dry mustard

1½ teaspoons salt

1. Prepare topping: Melt butter and in a bowl stir together with cheese until combined well. Topping may be made 1 day ahead and chilled, covered.

2. Heat oven to 400°. Butter a 3-quart shallow baking dish. Fill a 6-quart kettle three-quarters full with salted water and bring to boiling for macaroni.

3. Prepare sauce: In a 5-quart heavy saucepan melt butter over moderately low heat and stir in flour. Cook mixture, stirring, for 3 minutes. Remove from heat and whisk in milk. Return to heat and bring sauce to boiling, whisking constantly. Reduce heat and simmer 3 minutes, whisking occasionally. Stir in cheese, mustard, and salt. Remove pan from heat.

4. Cook macaroni in boiling water just until al dente. Reserve ½ cup cooking water and drain macaroni in colander. In a large bowl stir together macaroni, reserved cooking water, and sauce. Transfer mixture to baking dish.

5. Sprinkle topping evenly over macaroni and bake in middle of oven 20 to 25 minutes, or until golden and bubbling. For a crunchier crust, broil 3 minutes, or until crust is lightly browned.

Makes 6 (main-dish) servings.

Old-Fashioned Meat Loaf

8   ounces ground chuck

4   ounces ground pork

4   ounces ground veal

¼   cup grated onion

4   tablespoons chopped fresh parsley

3   tablespoons chili sauce

2   tablespoons Worcestershire sauce

     Salt and black pepper

1. Heat oven to 350°. In a large bowl, mix meats together until just combined. Place remaining ingredients in bowl. Toss together lightly.

2. Form meat mixture into an oval loaf in a small baking pan. Bake 50 minutes, or until cooked through. Do not overcook.

Makes 4 servings.

"Mothers have to remember what food each child likes or dislikes, which one is allergic to penicillin and hamster fur, who gets carsick and who isn't kidding when he stands outside the bathroom door and tells you what's going to happen if he doesn't get in right away. It's tough. If they all have the same hair color they tend to run together."

Erma Bombeck

SOURCES

Diane Ackerman, *A Natural History of the Senses* (Random House) Colette, "My Mother's House," in *My Mother's House* and *Sido,* trans. Una Vicenzo Troubridge and Enid McLeod (Farrar, Straus, and Giroux) Jill Ker Conway, *The Road From Coorain* (Knopf) Annie Dillard, *An American Childhood* (Harper Collins) Annie Ernaux, *A Woman's Story* (Quartet) Mia Farrow, *What Falls Away* (Bantam Doubleday Dell) Mary Karr, *The Liar's Club: A Memoir* (Viking Press) Jennifer Lauck, *Blackbird: A Childhood Lost and Found* (Atria Books) Barry Lopez, *About This Life: Journeys on the Threshold of Memory* (Random House) Tovah Martin, *A Time to Blossom* (Houghton Mifflin) Carson McCullers, *Illumination and Night Glare: The Unfinished Autobiography of Carson McCullers,* ed. Carlos L. Dews (University of Wisconsin Press) Anna Quindlen, *Living Out Loud* (Random House) Ruth Reichl, *Tender at the Bone* (Random House) Wallace Stegner, "Letter, Much Too Late," in *Where the Bluebird Sings to the Lemonade Springs: Living and Writing in the West* (Modern Library) "The Old Fashioned Mother" in *Treasury of Thought: Mother, Home, and Heaven,* compiled by Rosella Thorne (Bryan, Taylor, and Co) Rebecca Wells, *Divine Secrets of the Ya-Ya Sisterhood* (HarperCollins)